DOING BUSINESS WITH RESPECT AND INTEGRITY

A Step-By-Step Guide for Network Marketers

NAVELETTE WALKER

Table of Contents

Acknowledgements

I firstly want to thank God the merciful saviour for giving me the strength and tenacity to put my thoughts in this book to share with you the reader.

I would also like to thank my friend and partner Krystof Kapral who has been so patient with me all these years. My friend Althea Legister for showing me how it's done. Chantel Smith also a friend and mentor who is always encouraging and insightful.

A special thanks to Lloyd Montague who taught me the importance of working on self and for all the books, videos and recordings he bought and introduced me to.

To all my other friends and family members who came into my life to encourage and teach me the lessons I need to learn, I truly appreciate you all.

Introduction

"Give a man a fish and you feed him for a day; teach a man to fish and you feed him for a lifetime."

Lao Tsu

That's my life motto. I have always believed this quote and have proved it throughout my career as a Teacher, the best way to feed a person is to teach them how to do something rather than doing it for them. When we come into this world our parents and/or guardians teach us the do's and don'ts of life and as we learn and grow and go to nursery, school, college and the likes where we learn how to do different things and in the doing, we find what we like and don't like to do.

We are also taught to go to school, college and/or university and then get a good job working for someone else to feed ourselves and our family, but no one taught us how to do it for ourselves which I believe is the best way to ensure financial freedom, do it for yourself.

Network Marketing companies enable people to build a business which they can leave in their Wills for their children and their children's children. Yes, of course, you have to put in the work to enable your success and you would be doing the same thing as an employee but you will be building someone else's dream and not your own.

I have found that people are so attached to the Employee mindset of working for someone else that pays them just enough each week, fortnight and/or month for them to come back. And when you talk to them about Network Marketing they will ask, "is it a pyramid scheme?" I find this question laughable for the obvious reasons. According to Eric Worre a Network Marketing professional and leader, "Network Marketing isn't perfect. It's just better."

And I am of the same opinion, Network Marketing allows you to not only create wealth for yourself and your family, it also gives you the time needed to spend with your family and most importantly your children something which I believe many people who work for an employer don't have, hence, the way our society is today, children not feeling loved and nurtured as they should because mummy and daddy is out working for someone else.

You do the maths, having time to spend with your children and the opportunity to build wealth or working for someone making just enough to keep your head above water, I know which one I prefer.

The little sum you pay to join a Network Marketing company doesn't give it the respect it deserves, look at it this way, if you were to set up on your own, how much money would you need? And is success guaranteed? The answer to the latter question is no, as this book will illustrate.

Chapter 1

Getting Started

Research

Network Marketing (NM) is a good option if you are interested in starting a business and do not have the money needed to set-up on your own or you feel afraid to do business by yourself. If you find a good company which has all the tools you would need to get going quickly and easily it's a great opportunity that enables you to work for yourself but, not by yourself.

When I say Network Marketing (NM), I mean a company which has a system that duplicates with a product to sell/promote i.e. education, health and wellness, beauty etc. And a compensation plan, and you pay a one-off fee to join with no additional monthly charge except for the products you use, samples and literature needed to run your business.

Before you join any Network Marketing company there are a few things you should consider before going ahead and sign on the dotted line and these are.

Product(s)

➤ What is the product(s)?
➤ Does these product(s) help people? If so, in what way does it help people?

- What do I like about the business concept?
- Would I use the product(s)?

Team

- Do they love the company?
- Do they love the product(s)?
- Do they use the product(s)?
- Do they have integrity?
- Are they open and honest?
- Will they be there to teach and encourage you daily, if necessary?
- Is there any company politics which you could get caught up in?
- Can they stop you from achieving the goals you set for yourself?
- Do they have barriers that can stop you from achieving your personal goals? I.e. you need a license to do the business.
- Do they have written policies and procedures in place which you need to adhere to?
- Are these policies and procedures accessible by you?
- Can you see yourself working harmoniously with them?
- Do you have the same goals? (Extremely important).
- Has anyone in the team achieved any levels above the Manager level?

System

- Is there a duplicable system in place?
- How easy is it to duplicate?
- What type of system is it? Generic or scripted?

> ➢ What type of training is given? And how frequently is it given?
> ➢ Where does the training take place?
> ➢ Can you afford to go to training weekly, if necessary? (Due to distance).
> ➢ Is it an "us and them" type of a company?
> ➢ Or is it "we sing from the same hymn sheet" type of a company?

Compensation Plan

> ➢ How much can you earn at each level?
> ➢ How difficult is it to achieve those levels?

I joined both of these companies, the generic and scripted with the us and them culture versus the "we sing from the same hymn sheet" company and have found the latter to be the best, in that, when the whole company is singing from the same hymn sheet and everything is scripted it makes it easier to follow and duplicate and at the same time enable you to advance quickly in the company, thus, allowing you to become an outright business owner where you are greatly rewarded for your efforts, based on your teams' performance sooner rather than later.

A generic system is one which has a continuous personal recruitment and sales target each month with no scripts for making calls so when you make calls you are pretty much winging it. There are also weekly training, one from the company where invitees (potential recruits) are shown how the business works and one with your team which is run by an Upline on the intricacies of the business. There are also other training which you will be charged for.

A scripted system is where you also have recruitment and sales targets each month and everything is scripted, from making recruitment and sales call to closing a deal and you have training on a weekly basis, sometimes twice a week, one from the company which teaches about recruitment, sales, closing etc. And the other from your Upline who will teach about products, updates, systems and so on. And one for invitees (potential recruits). You may also have one-to-one training from your sponsor (the person who recruited you).

Taking the time to research the above and the team you sign-up into is of paramount importance, something I failed to do on both occasions and lived to regret my choices.

The first team I signed up into was in the generic system company where there were no scripts to refer to which meant we were making things up as we went along and this was not duplicable, thus, making it hard to achieve anything without extremely hard work. It wasn't all bad, I learnt a great deal from this experience and I write this book so you don't have to make the same mistakes.

In this team, I excelled quickly due to my determination to succeed and from the help and support gained from my Upline's Sponsor and not my direct Upline.

He would buy and send me links to books to read and listen to, as well as, meet with me daily to help me build my business, however, to get to the next level was extremely hard because the 17 people I had recruited did nothing so, I had to continue recruiting to find people that were as hungry as I was for success, then I gave up because I realise that I couldn't duplicate what I had learnt and many other factors which I do not wish to disclose here.

The few team members that tried to do the business couldn't overcome their fear of talking to people they did not know and this is a skill anyone who wants to be successful in Network Marketing has to learn and master.

I loved the products in both companies and I used them so, it was easy for me to be enthusiastic about sharing them with others because I felt that people needed to know about them.

I would advise you to use the products yourself to see if you get any adverse reaction from them, I say this because I had an enthusiastic team member who could not use the products because she was allergic to the main ingredients in the products, and how do you promote or sell something you cannot use? However, she tried but gave up in the end.

The second company I joined is what I call the scripted company, there were scripts for everything making it so much easier to move quickly in the business, these scripts was what the generic company didn't have which made it twice as hard to do that business, however, here I was in my element until I was going for what we call the Supervisor position and got slowed down due to lies and dishonesty.

My Sponsor kept telling me you can't do this, you can't do that because you are not licensed, why? Because the longer she followed me around without my license rather than make my training to get my license a priority, the more money she would make from me and the team which I recruited.

This is why I emphasize that you do your research and your due diligence before joining any Network Marketing company, their goal was not my goal. I joined the business to help people first because I knew that the money would come if I just focus on helping people, however, my Sponsor's goal was to make money and she saw everyone that came into her team as pound signs £, literally!

It got to the point where I had to write to the CEO asking for a transfer from this team, it was awful. I stress again please, please, please research and research some more before you join any NM company and especially the team you are thinking about signing up into.

If it takes a month or two to carry out your research then so be it, do not feel pressure from anyone asking you to join their team, block them if you have to until, you feel you have sufficient information to make an informed decision because some of these people are pushy beyond belief and can become a pest, stand firm and keep a level head. They are just thinking about their monthly target and not you.

The checklist above is there to help you with your research of the company and the team you are thinking of joining; there may be additional research you may need to carry out such as, how long the company has been around and are they registered and regulated by the regulatory body they claim to be regulated by.

These checks can be carried out by doing a search on the Company House website and any other regulator websites they mention in the business overview which, they invite you to at the beginning of the process. If they don't mention the regulators, ask the person who invited you to the business overview.

Even if the person who invited you to the business overview is a family member or a really good friend, still carry out these checks yourself because they may be new to the organisation and did not carry out these checks themselves.

It is better to be safe than sorry.

Chapter 2

The missing link

"Personal development — the never-ending chance to improve not only yourself, but also attract opportunities and affect others."

Jim Rohn.

Personal Development

Read

I mentioned in the previous chapter that I learnt a lot from my experience in the generic company and I also stated that my Upline's Sponsor would buy and send me links to books to read and listen to, there was a reason for this and I would say this is the most difficult part of becoming self-employed or a Network Marketer, why? Many people overlook this part and eventually fail in business because we are bought up being told that we need to go to School, College and/or University, get good grades so we can get a good job at the end of it all.

When we go into business this is the programme which we have running in our subconscious mind and we need to replace this programme when we go into business whether we go into business by ourselves or in the Network Marketing arena.

Personal Development (PD) would replace what they call Continuous Professional Development (CPD) in the workplace, you are now in business so, you need to work on yourself to enable you to grow and attract the right people to your business. You will need to read good books like Acres of Diamonds, one of my favourite books and others such as.

> How To Win Friends and Influence People – Dale Carnegie
> The Power of Your Subconscious Mind – Dr Joseph Murphy
> Go Pro, 7 Steps To Becoming A Network Marketing Professional – Eric Worre
> How Successful People Grow – John C Maxwell
> Thinking for a Change – John C Maxwell
> The Magic of Believing – Claude Bristol
> Rich Dad, Poor Dad – Robert T Kiyosaki
> Think and Grow Rich – Napoleon Hill

I have written this list in the order of importance based on my experience of reading from this list. I feel it best to read as listed above, this will become apparent to you as you go through this list of books and this is by no means an exhaustive list and if you are anything like me who love books and reading, you will find that you will add to this list as you learn and grow, and thirst for more knowledge on personal development.

Many motivational speakers and business coaches will tell you to read ten pages of a good book every day after you wake up and listen to something motivational in your sleepy state, I will cover this in more detail later.

Most of the books listed above can be found in written and audio form, choose what works best for you. Ensure that you follow the principles in this chapter because missing this section can either make you or break you. This chapter may be the hardest to do but it will pay dividends in the long run.

Why is this chapter's instructions the hardest? Because many people find it hard to pick up a book to read whether in written or audio form, as one of my team members said to me when I told her about the importance of reading and working on one's self, "I have read enough throughout my life, what do I need to do that for?" And she refused to read or do any personal development, thus, found the business very hard to do and she gave up before achieving anything.

As John Heywood states, "Rome was not built in a day, but they were laying bricks every hour." Many people go into business after working for someone else and have that same Employee mindset and they expect quick rewards for doing little or nothing at all. Whether you go into business by yourself or in an NM company, business requires hard work before any real profit is made. Statistics show that many new businesses fail in the first five years.

"It's often said that more than half of new businesses fail during the first year. According to the Small Business Association (SBA), this isn't necessarily true. The SBA states that only 30% of new businesses fail during the first two years of being open, 50% during the first five years and 66% during the first 10." https://www.investopedia.com/financial-edge/1010/top-6-reasons-new-businesses-fail.aspx.

I believe that many businesses fail because business owners skip the important part, Personal Development, there could be other reasons as well but I think this plays a major role. Don't take my word for it try, it for yourself and keep me posted on your findings.

I can be contacted at info@navelettewalker.com.

Listen to something motivational (before getting out of Bed)

The other part of personal development as mentioned earlier is to listen to something motivational as soon as you wake up out of your slumber, this is because your subconscious mind is in the Theta brain wave state and is more open to suggestions/change in this state.

"Every part of your body vibrates to its own rhythm. Your brain has a unique set of brain waves. In neuroscience, there are five distinct brain wave frequencies, namely Beta, Alpha, Theta, Delta and the lesser-known Gamma. Learning mind control at the deeper states of consciousness opens you up to the world of your subconscious mind where you can create your reality at will and with exact precision." https://www.mind-your-reality.com/brain_waves.html.

The following lists are motivational speakers and successful Network Marketers who I personally listen to.

> Art Williams
> Les Brown
> Zig Ziglar
> Jim Rohn
> John C. Maxwell

➤ Brian Tracey

Again, this is by no means an exhaustive list of motivational speakers and successful Network Marketers, I am sure you will find more as you learn and grow. I use the list above because they work for me. Most if not all of the above can be found on YouTube.

Keep healthy

The final part of personal development is exercise, eating well and getting a good night's rest, after all, you wouldn't want to become a six or seven figure earner and not have good health to enjoy the fruits of your labour, would you?

It would be presumptuous of me to tell you what exercise you should do, what kind of food you should eat or what time you should go to sleep, I will leave this up to you. I can, however, share my regime with you.

When I wake up and before I get out of bed I pick up my mobile phone and head to YouTube to listen to one of the Speakers mentioned above, I then drink a glass of water which I usually have waiting on my Bedside Table and then I head to the Bathroom.

After doing my morning Bathroom routine, I make a cup of coffee and then I read or listen to one of the books mentioned earlier, then I exercise for about 15 - 20 minutes and then go back to the kitchen to make myself a Smoothie it could be Banana or Strawberry, and I may have some Oats Porridge later.

I may or may not take some Vitamins, but I ensure that I drink plenty of water throughout the day to keep hydrated. My Lunch and evening meals are varied so not much to say about that but they will almost always have some kind of carbs and vegetables included. I do try to get a minimum of 8 hours sleep but sometimes I read throughout the night and I am not suggesting that you do this, this is my routine.

The more time you spend on personal development the easier your business will become and the more successful you will be, as I mentioned earlier, this is the hardest part of the business which is why so many business owners ignore it and live to tell the tale about their many business ventures that failed.

You will find many people who have tried Network Marketing and will tell you, "It doesn't work." But I can tell you that it does if you follow the instructions in this book and do the work necessary to enable your success.

Think of this chapter as your new religion for business success and if you are religious, you can add the Bible, Torah, Koran etc. to your reading list and some gospel music or its equivalence as your motivational piece before you get out of bed.

Chapter 3

Get Stuck In

Planning

Now that you have worked on yourself it's time to plan for business success. The following table is an example of a weekly planner you may want to create for yourself or you can use a diary or a daily planner.

WEEKLY PLANNER

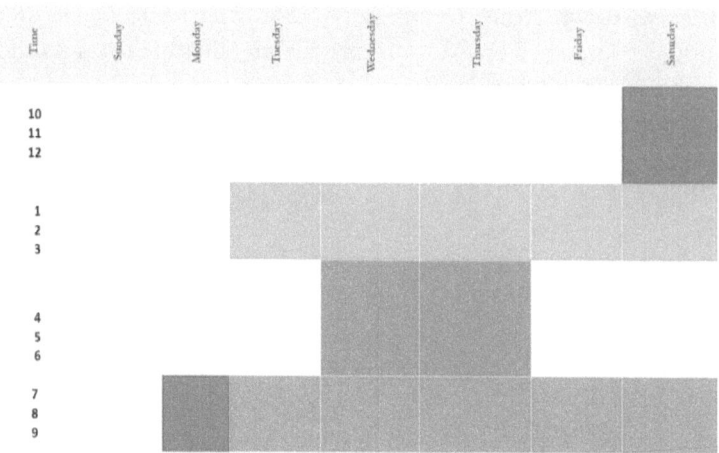

KEY:

> BLUE = DOING 1-2-1 WITH TEAM MEMBERS
> RED = ATTENDING TRAINING
> GREEN = MAKING RECRUITMENT CALLS
> WHITE = MONEY MAKING ACTIVITIES (PERSONAL COLOUR OF YOUR CHOICE).

Creating a plan of what you do on a daily bases is imperative to your success. Creating a plan of the steps you will take to build your business will keep you focused and ensure you start building quickly so you can start earning.

There are different types of NM companies i.e. education, health and wellness, beauty, clothing etc. and they will all have similar systems but you may have to do some studying to get a license to practice like me in the second company.

Your Upline may take advantage of you not having a license and slow down your progress by not providing the 1-2-1 training you need to enable you moving as quickly as you would like because s/he can make more money out of you and the team members you recruit. This is why it is important that you take time to do your research on the team you join before signing up.

Calling Prospects

Let's assume you have done your research and you have a good Sponsor and/or Upline and they want it for you as much as you want it for yourself. You plan your week and start making your recruitment calls from the list of people you know.

The people you know will not be your target but the people they know. When you call them you are not saying, "I have joined this great company and would like you to come and take a look," rather you will call them and say, "Who do you know who is ambitious and hardworking and is looking for an opportunity to make an extra £... per month, working ...hours per week?" And you wait for the person's answer. (This information should be given to you by your Sponsor and/or Upline).

Some will say, "I know me." You say, "That's great I will take your details, but who else do you know?"

Make sure to have a notepad and pen with you when you are making the calls to take down the name, telephone number etc. of the people or person they will give to you and don't forget to take their details too if they told you that they are interested too.

You will need their first and last name (surname), telephone number and email address because you may need to put these details in a system to send them an invitation to a business overview. At the start of your journey in Network Marketing your only job is to recruit your team members so, your main focus should be getting people to agree to meet you at the business overview and you use the system to send out the invitations, if necessary.

When I made calls to invite people to the business overview my focus was on the daily target that I had set for myself. I would get a glass of water, my notepad and pen and I would plug my headset into my mobile and start making my calls with the intention of getting three people to say YES to me by the end of my daily calling sessions. At first, it took me two hours to get those three YESES but, by being consistent on a daily basis those two hours reduced.

If they ask, "What is it?" "What will I be doing?" You tell them what type of company it is i.e. "We are an education company, we teach people how to…" Or whatever it is your company do, it is not for you to do a presentation over the telephone, you are making the calls to invite them to a business overview where all the necessary information about the business will be covered, you are not an expert yet, leave that to the experts and focus on getting three YESES per day. If you do this and stick to it no matter what happens on the day of the business overview, you will start building your business quickly, even if only one person shows up to the business overview.

The first week I started this process I got 13 YESES and only one person showed up because I didn't know how to use the system for sending out the invitations, and I sent them the actual form for them to complete themselves which, was my job to do, however, the one person that showed up signed up one week later.

The following week I got 19 YESES and eight people showed up and none signed up, and then the next week after that I had 16 YESES and only one showed up, and he signed up 3 days later.

And a friend who came to my business overview with me signed up a few weeks after I had signed up. This made three team members who had now put me in the position to go for the Supervisor's position, all I had to do was complete my final assessment to get my license and sell some products to make the monetary target set by the company and I am a Supervisor who now gets 50% of everything I sell and so on.

I also had a week where I had 13 YESES and no one showed up.

Many people come into Network Marketing and it doesn't matter how much training and one-to-one help they get, they are afraid to pick up the phone and make the calls necessary to get them what they want. What's the worst that can happen from picking up the phone and calling someone to ask, "Who do you know...?" In my experience, the worst that happened was people telling me ...

- o They would call me back and never did.
- o They will send me a list and never did.
- o It's not for me.
- o Call me back - and when I called them back at the agreed time, they wouldn't pick up the phone.

All of those were people's way of saying I am not interested right now or they may never be interested but, my focus was on who needs my help right now and when I got any of the above statements, I would say ok, it isn't you and I continue to say out loud as I am making the calls, "Father, who in this list needs my help today?" Until I got my three YESES for that day. Sometimes you will get 4 or 5 yeses because someone wants to bring a friend along as I did.

I brought two friends to my business overview and one signed up into my team a few weeks later after I had signed up. Yes, I know I mentioned this earlier. It's just a reminder for you to bring some friends along with you.

I hope I have shown you that you have nothing to fear about picking up your phone and making those calls? As Art Williams would say, "Just do it, and do it." If you keep doing this on a daily basis, it will become one of your greatest skills.

It's about consistent and persistent efforts so go ahead and build that muscle, you will be glad you did.

The Business Overview

After you have made your calls and got your YESES for the week, for the next business overview, you will need to send out the invitations, please learn the system for sending out invitations and if you are not sure how to do it ask your Sponsor or Upline, don't make the same mistake I made.

Depending on the NM Company you may want to sit in on the meeting with your guests or if available attend another training session to learn how to do the business and wait for the business overview to finish before meeting with your guests, and introduce them to your Upline for the follow-up meeting.

Under no circumstances should you be the one to do the follow-up meeting unless you are trained to do so, of course when you get to the manager position you will be able to do this for you and your team members because you will have enough experience by then.

The idea here is for you to learn the business as you go, it is more important to TAKE ACTION to enable you moving quickly and start making money after all that's the reason why most people join a Network Marketing company.

I joined for many reasons, first to help people, second to become independent of Employers and finally to become financially independent. Your WHY? may differ, if you focus and do the work it will work for you. It's all in the doing.

Chapter 4

Duplicate

Train your team members

In an ideal world, it would be great if we could do everything ourselves to become a success, but life really doesn't work like that you are only one person with one pair of hands and can only get so much done in a day by yourself, you need people to build a successful business whether in network marketing or a business of your own. It is, therefore, important to recruit and teach people to do the same thing that you did to become successful. We call this duplicating yourself in network marketing.

I am a great believer that people don't do what you say, but what you do, you need to be the example for your team do not expect them to do what you wouldn't do. According to Lewis Cass, "People may doubt what you say, but they will believe what you do." Be the example for your team. Not everyone you recruit will be ready to do the business when they come in so don't try to push them, let them be they will do it when they or ready or not at all. But leave the door open for them for when they are ready.

Focus on the people who are doing something, some may work in silence and will very rarely contact you, but you will see the fruits of their labour, contact them from time to time to see how they are doing and if there is anything they need. Even if they say no, invite them out for a coffee and praise them for what they are doing, this will encourage them to continue what they are doing.

Others may need your help so, you need to help them in any way you can i.e. take them out with you so they can shadow what you do and/or team them up with another team member who is doing well and doesn't mind showing someone else what to do. Please remember you are not their employer, they are in the same boat as you, wanting something different from what life has fed them so far.

Treat team members with respect

You may be your team members Sponsor or Upline, but refrain from using the hierarchy BS on your team members, most of them have had a career before this and was successful in that career and even though network marketing is new to them, they have a lot of transferrable skills for this business, please respect and acknowledge that.

I have had Sponsors and Uplines who use this hierarchy BS on me and it really didn't sit well with me, I even had a Sponsor telling me that my Assessor skills cannot be used in this business, I said nothing but this offended me so much I had no respect for her. If you are a qualified Assessor you can, in fact, assess anything which you have experience in, for example, if you have experience as an Administrator and have an Assessor's qualification, you can assess the Business Administration qualification but, I couldn't be bothered to explain this to her due to her arrogance.

Respect is earned and not given. So what if you got to the manager's position in two months? Teach them how to do the same, they will respect you for it. No one likes a smart ass.

Support team members

As I mentioned earlier, in some NM companies a license may be required to enable you to do the business and you will need to go out with your team members and deliver for them while they watch you, and then you will need to assess them doing the same thing to enable them getting their license.

A word of advice, you may want to make the calls for your new team members to get the appointments, but I would advise you to meet with them in person or online and teach them how to make the calls themselves whilst you observe and give them feedback following each call.

I advise you to do this because if you don't and you make the calls for your team members and you do not have the time to give them updates on what is happening regularly, this does and will cause suspicion and your team members may think that you are rude and wonder what you are doing with their list of potential clients and/or recruits.

Some Sponsors and Uplines like to ask new team members to email a list of people they know to them which is used to assess how coachable the new team members are and a lot of people become very suspicious when they are asked for the list and then very rarely hear from the Sponsor or Upline after they have sent the list.

This is because the Sponsor and/or Upline do not call them until they have some news for the new team member this, in my opinion, this is bad practice and should be changed to sending the form required for completion to the new team member, then arrange to meet up with the new team member to make the calls.

This way you both know what is happening and can synchronise your diaries for those appointments rather than you taking the list, making the appointments and then calling your team member to tell them about the appointments you have made for them, without checking that they are available on those dates and times.

I experienced the above and had to make changes to my plans because I really wanted to get my business up and running, but as I said, do not make your new team members feel this way it is not professional and it is rude to assume that people haven't got other things to do.

When people join a network marketing company it's because they want a change from what they are used to and may still have a full-time job and will need time to adjust their diary and their mindset for the business, as I mentioned in earlier chapters most people have the employee programme running when they join a network marketing company and will need time to adjust to the new way of doing things and patience is, therefore, needed as well as gentle encouragement.

Of course, there are people who want to get started right away and you should be prepared for that because you may not be paying attention when a new team member is demonstrating that they want to move quickly.

When I started in the second company I wanted to get started right away and demonstrated this by completing my online assessment in three days but, my Sponsor failed to recognise my eagerness to get started even though I attended training every week and brought a potential recruit with me. She failed to see the urgency I had and didn't think it important to help me get my license as quickly as possible, so much so, we had continuous disagreements because I became suspicious as to why she was dragging her feet.

I believed it to be that the longer she followed me and my team members around, the more money she could make because she had a limited mindset and didn't see the business the way that I saw it, that is, for every one number I had there is a sea of people available to me, and she seemed to see me and my team members as her bank, and rather than do some recruiting for herself, she would take my team members' list too and I didn't make any money from my team members but, she did.

She would say, "You cannot meet with the team members you are not licensed."

My point is, don't let greed cloud your judgement do your business with integrity and have respect for others. This is not a job, it is people going into business to enable a better life, treat your team members as you would like to be treated. Be selfless and you will be greatly rewarded.

Chapter 5

What does it take to be successful in Network Marketing?

"Success is nothing more than a few simple disciplines, practised every day."

Jim Rohn.

Stage 1

It begins with you, as mentioned in chapter two the hardest part of this business is Personal Development but, doing it ensures a better experience throughout the journey.

Network Marketing is all about dealing with people, from the customers to your team members. You will need to recruit team members and duplicate yourself by showing them how to do what you have done to get to whatever position you are in i.e. Supervisor, Manager etc.

We all want to attract the best people to our team and the fastest way to do that is to make Personal Development your priority. It can be a painful experience when you first begin because you are no longer looking out but, looking within and things you weren't aware of about yourself will come up and you may want to run for the hills but stick with it, I promise, it will get easier.

You will pick up one of the books mentioned in chapter two to read and you will put it down and forget about it because you are not ready for that message, it took me two years to read, "How to Win Friends and Influence People." because I picked it up and looked at the title and thought, this person wants me to learn how to manipulate people, but once I finally read it, I wish I had read it years earlier and I read it three times back to back.

My Upline's Sponsor in the first company introduced me to some of these books and motivation speakers but I had been listening to Les Brown for years. I would sit up throughout the night and read books after books and listen to motivation speakers back to back, then I would go to bed around 5.00 am, wake up around 12.00 pm, shower, dress and leave to meet my Upline's Sponsor for 1.30 pm to learn the skills necessary to do the business such as how to approach someone and get their telephone number, how to do a one-to-one presentation and sign someone up on the spot.

This practice became easier as I worked on myself and practised the skills, and it will work for you too and no, I am not suggesting that you read and listen to motivation speakers until 5.00 am in the morning that was my practice. I believe I covered a more practical routine in the Personal Development chapter.

Stage 2

The next thing is to learn the system within your organisation and the compensation plan, most compensation plan will tell you what you need to do to get into each position within the company and the potential earnings possible at each stage.

Stage 3

Focus on building your team, depending on the company you join, you may or may not be able to work with your team members, a word of advice If you need a license to do the business don't build your team until you get it. Focus on getting your license before making the phone calls to invite people to the business overview, instead, call people (customers) to help you get your license because without it you earn less and you will not be able to work with your team members.

Stage 4

Once you move to the next position in the company teach your team members how to do the same, in other words, duplicate yourself and work deep and wide in your team, help your team members' team members and so on. Don't leave anything to chance.

In-Network Marketing companies you will have monthly sales targets so build, develop and maintain your customer base, take care of your customers and they will take care of you by referring other people to you. Create a referral system in your business don't see one person as just one person, see each person you talk to as a network of people because they have friends, work colleagues and family members who may be interested in your business and your products so build a relationship with everyone you meet. Read, "How to Win Friends and Influence People." It will help you with this.

Note: when you are ready to recruit your team members, you will find your first set in your mobile phone and not from a list of people you met at a networking event, on the bus or in the Supermarket, those people will join you later as you find creative ways to build and develop a relationship with them, like remembering their Birthday and sending them a handwritten card if you know their address or if not, a nice text or WhatsApp message.

DO, LEARN AND TEACH! And success will be yours. Like life, you will have good days and bad days that's life, "just do it, and do it."

If not available, create the following table to plan your goals/why? for going into Network Marketing it will keep you focused if you know why you are doing it.

Development Plan

Planned outcome:

Where do I want to be by the end of this period? What do I want to be doing?
NAME:

COVERING THE PERIOD FROM:		TO:	DATE:
What do I want to achieve?	What resources or support will I need?	What will my success criteria be?	Target dates for review and completion

About the Author

When I was younger I had many dreams and wanted to do many things, but I always knew that I would become a teacher because I did it in school, I helped my maths teacher teach my classmates and found it enjoyable.

Before going into education as a teacher there were other job experiences I wanted to have such as being a Beauty Consultant, Accounts Clerk and Secretary and I did them all before finally doing the thing I believe I was created to do, teach, and I have spent the past 23 years teaching various courses from ICT to Internal Quality Assurance in further education.

I enjoyed my teaching experience but, it wasn't providing the things I so longed to have, like a beautiful house of my own and being able to drive any car I wanted. When I discovered a better way to teach and earn the kind of money that would enable me to do the things I wanted, I jumped all over it because it was a no brainer for me.

I now focus on creating and building a business that allows me to enjoy life and achieve the things I want to.

Reference

Go Pro – 7 Steps to Becoming a Network Marketing Professional – Eric Worre

Inspirational quotes - Jim Rohn, Lewis Cass and John Heywood

Art William's Just do it, and do it video - YouTube

Lao Tsu quotes - Lao Tsu

Brain Waves and the Deeper States of Consciousness - https://www.mind-your-reality.com/brain_waves.html

Top 6 Reasons New Businesses Fail - https://www.investopedia.com/financial-edge/1010/top-6-reasons-new-businesses-fail.aspx

Blank Intentionally